This Trip Tracker is the property of...

Name: _____

Address: _____

_____

_____

Phone
Number: _____

Birthday: _____

...So hands off!

Here's what I look like.

(Draw a picture or paste a photo here.)

I'm on my way to _____.

I'm traveling by _____

Trip Calendar

Here's my itinerary—where I'm going and when.

Month _____

Sun.	Mon.	Tues.	Wed.	Thurs.	Fri.	Sat.

I can't wait to see how things turn out!

As far as predictions go, I'm most looking forward to _____.

Cast of Characters

Here's the inside story on my travel companions.

NAME	RELATIONSHIP TO ME	WORD THAT BEST DESCRIBES THIS PERSON

I'm sure I'll have more to say about them later.

Getting Ready

Things to do before I leave:

- [ ] Read about places I'm going to visit.

- [ ] Check out these places on a map.

- [ ] Write to city and state tourist offices. (Lots of free stuff!)

- [ ] Fill out names and addresses in my journal. (Don't forget stamps!)

- [ ] Pack. (Maybe Mom or Dad will help me.)

- [ ] Say goodbye to my friends.

- [ ] Get really excited!

- [ ] _____

- [ ] _____

- [ ] _____

Packing Checklist

This is what I plan to bring on my trip.

Stuff to BRING

I've it PACKED

_____   _____
_____   _____
_____   _____
_____   _____
_____   _____
_____   _____
_____   _____
_____   _____
_____   _____
_____   _____
_____

The most important thing to remember to pack is my _____.

I never travel without it!

Keeping in Touch

These are some of the people I might write to on my trip.

- [ ] The President
- [ ] Best friend
- [ ] Neighbor
- [ ] Doctor
- [ ] Whoever wrote me last
- [ ] ~~Girlfriend or Boyfriend~~ FORGET IT!
- [ ] Pet
- [ ] Favorite stuffed animal

- [ ] Pizza delivery kid
- [ ] Teacher
- [ ] Parents
- [ ] Grandparents
- [ ] Aunts and Uncles
- [ ] Cousins
- [ ] Teammates
- [ ] Other_____

Don't forget a stamp. (Stamp out forgetfulness!)

name + address of person you're writing to

Date →
greeting →
message →
closing →
your name →

April 1, 2010
Dear Ima,
I'm having the most awesome, fantastic, coolest time ever! I hope your vacation has been just as great.
I'll see you soon,
Best regards,
Yuri Pal

Ima Friend
2 Yew St.
Anytown, Anyplace 12345

Get busy writing! Did you think you were on vacation or something?

Names and Addresses

I've put the names and addresses of old
and new friends here so I can write to them.

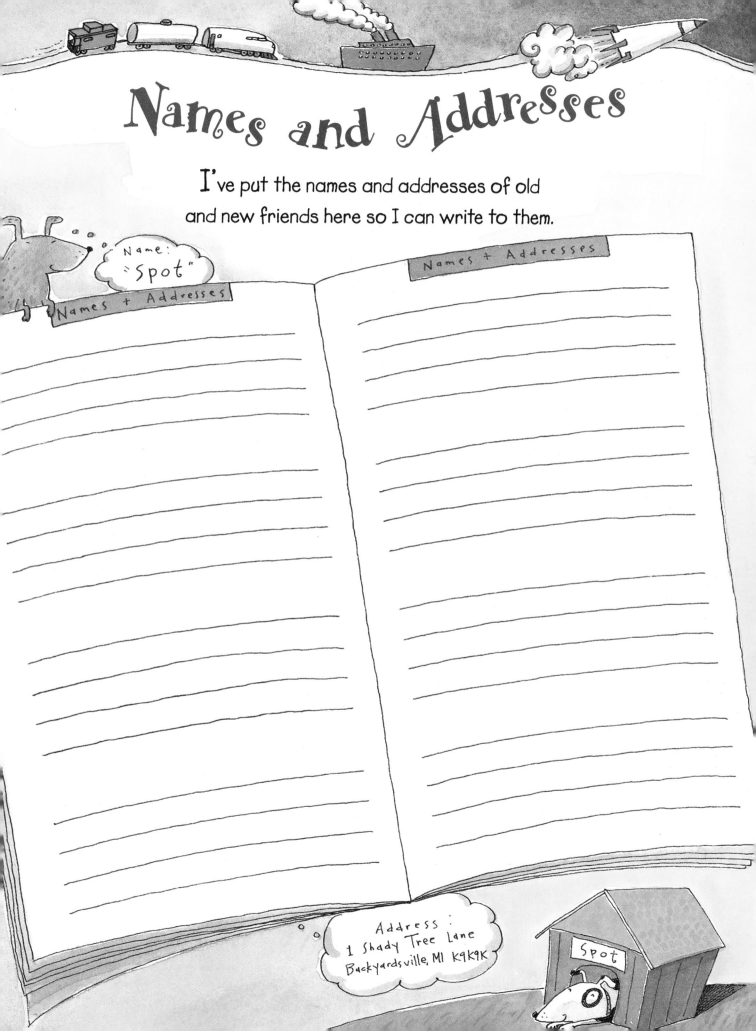

Name:
"Spot"

Names + Addresses

Names + Addresses

Address :
1 Shady Tree Lane
Backyardsville, MI K9K9K

Spot

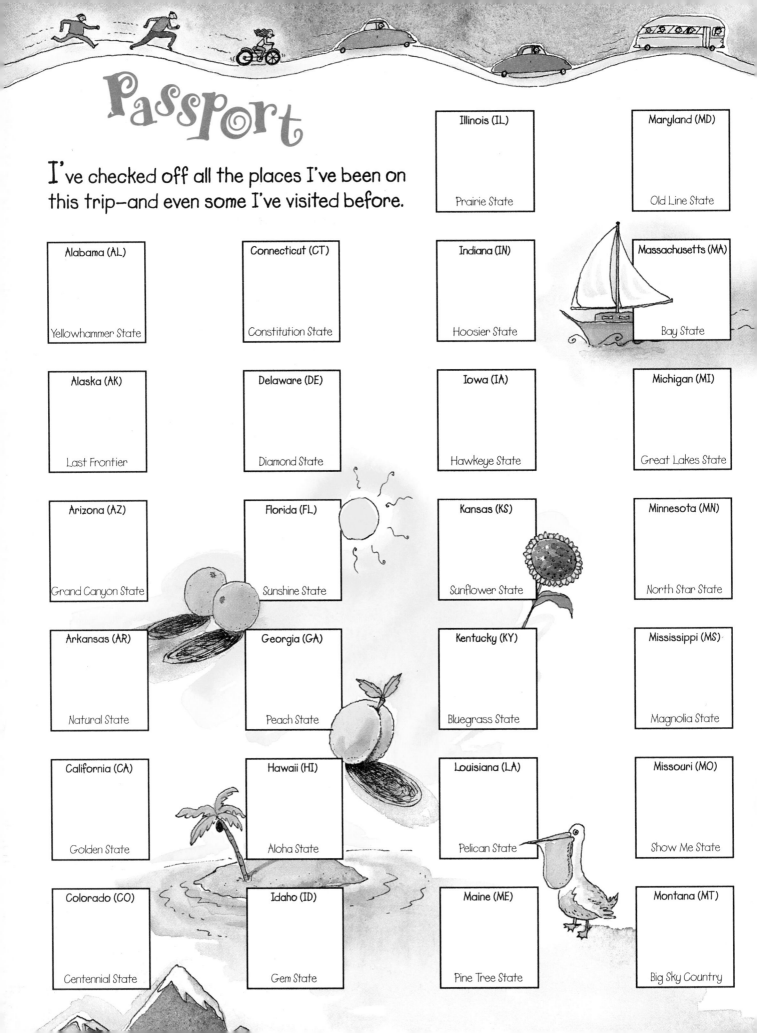

Passport

I've checked off all the places I've been on this trip—and even some I've visited before.

Illinois (IL) — Prairie State	**Maryland (MD)** — Old Line State	

Alabama (AL) — Yellowhammer State

Connecticut (CT) — Constitution State

Indiana (IN) — Hoosier State

Massachusetts (MA) — Bay State

Alaska (AK) — Last Frontier

Delaware (DE) — Diamond State

Iowa (IA) — Hawkeye State

Michigan (MI) — Great Lakes State

Arizona (AZ) — Grand Canyon State

Florida (FL) — Sunshine State

Kansas (KS) — Sunflower State

Minnesota (MN) — North Star State

Arkansas (AR) — Natural State

Georgia (GA) — Peach State

Kentucky (KY) — Bluegrass State

Mississippi (MS) — Magnolia State

California (CA) — Golden State

Hawaii (HI) — Aloha State

Louisiana (LA) — Pelican State

Missouri (MO) — Show Me State

Colorado (CO) — Centennial State

Idaho (ID) — Gem State

Maine (ME) — Pine Tree State

Montana (MT) — Big Sky Country

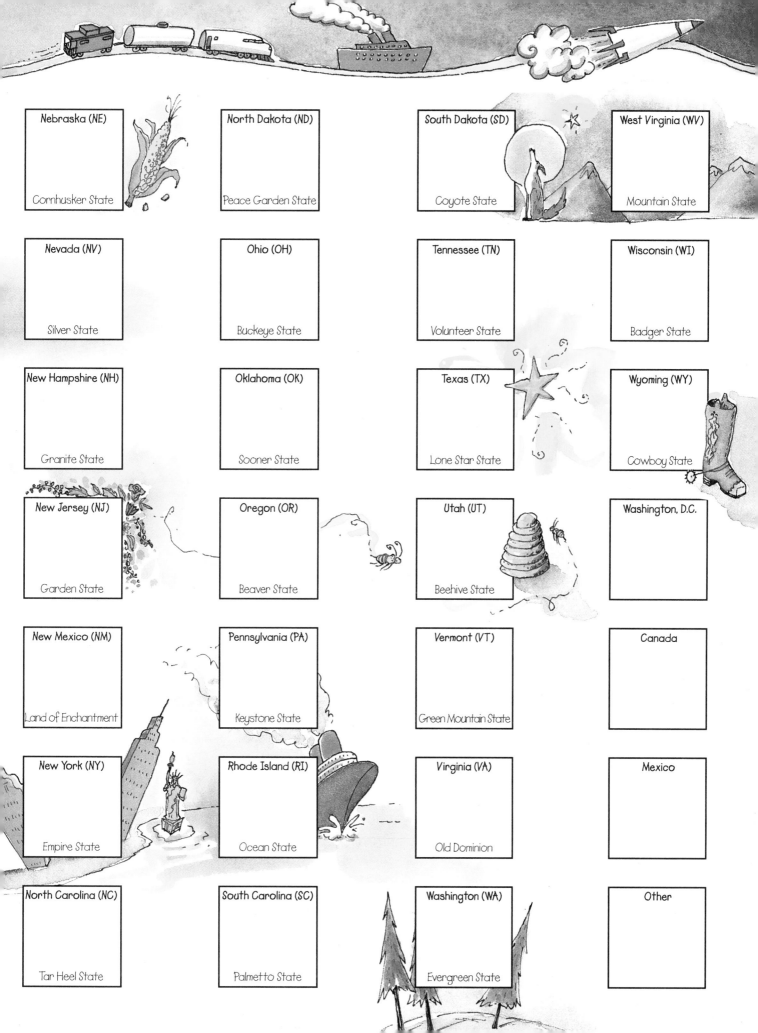

Nebraska (NE) Cornhusker State	North Dakota (ND) Peace Garden State	South Dakota (SD) Coyote State	West Virginia (WV) Mountain State
Nevada (NV) Silver State	Ohio (OH) Buckeye State	Tennessee (TN) Volunteer State	Wisconsin (WI) Badger State
New Hampshire (NH) Granite State	Oklahoma (OK) Sooner State	Texas (TX) Lone Star State	Wyoming (WY) Cowboy State
New Jersey (NJ) Garden State	Oregon (OR) Beaver State	Utah (UT) Beehive State	Washington, D.C.
New Mexico (NM) Land of Enchantment	Pennsylvania (PA) Keystone State	Vermont (VT) Green Mountain State	Canada
New York (NY) Empire State	Rhode Island (RI) Ocean State	Virginia (VA) Old Dominion	Mexico
North Carolina (NC) Tar Heel State	South Carolina (SC) Palmetto State	Washington (WA) Evergreen State	Other

U.S. Map

Time to hit the road—details to follow...

Travel Journal

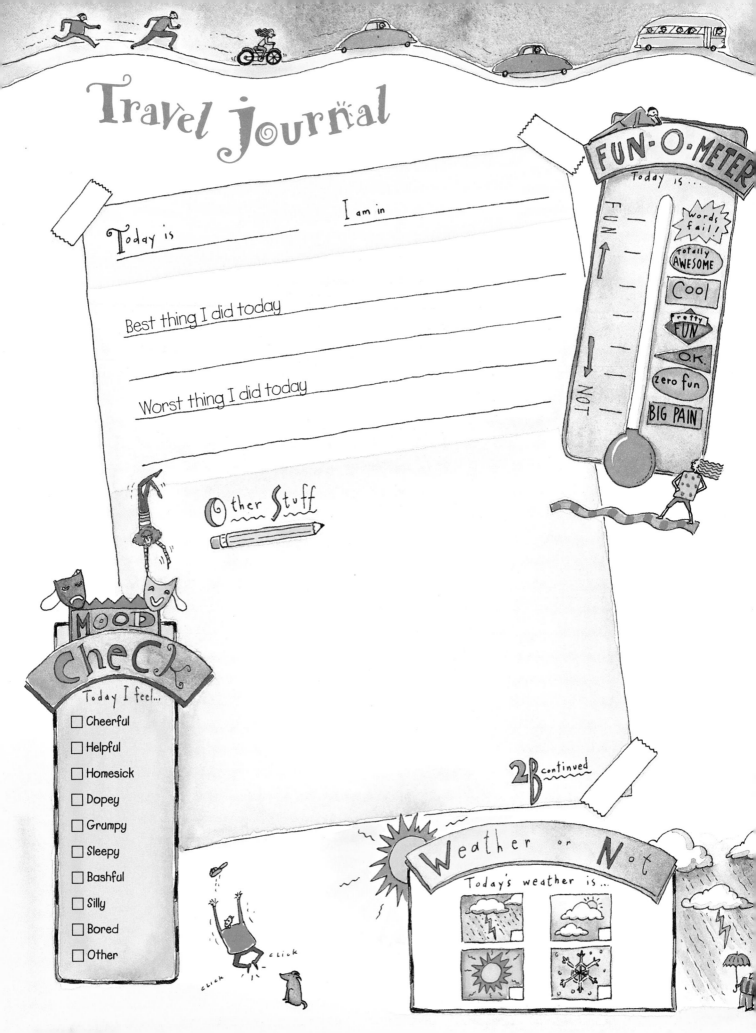

Today is _____   I am in _____

Best thing I did today _____

Worst thing I did today _____

Other Stuff

FUN-O-METER
Today is...

- words fail!
- totally AWESOME
- Cool
- pretty FUN
- O.K.
- zero fun
- BIG PAIN

MOOD CHECK
Today I feel...

- ☐ Cheerful
- ☐ Helpful
- ☐ Homesick
- ☐ Dopey
- ☐ Grumpy
- ☐ Sleepy
- ☐ Bashful
- ☐ Silly
- ☐ Bored
- ☐ Other

2B continued

Weather or Not
Today's weather is...

Travel tips

Here are some tips for an awesome trip.

Stake out your territory.

Show off your map-reading skills.

Here are some more...

Stay energized!

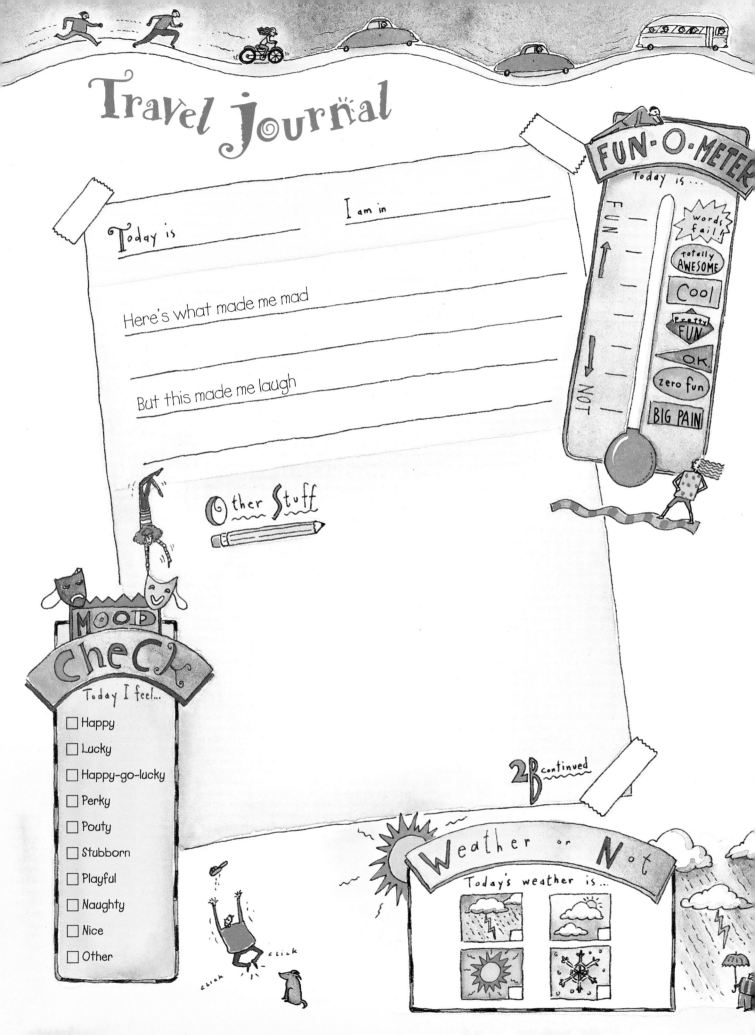

Travel Journal

Today is _____   I am in _____

Here's what made me mad _____

But this made me laugh _____

Other **St**uff

FUN-O-METER
Today is...

FUN
NOT

words fail!
totally AWESOME
Cool
Pretty FUN
OK
zero fun
BIG PAIN

MOOD CheCK
Today I feel...

☐ Happy
☐ Lucky
☐ Happy-go-lucky
☐ Perky
☐ Pouty
☐ Stubborn
☐ Playful
☐ Naughty
☐ Nice
☐ Other

2B continued

Weather or **Not**
Today's weather is...

click click click

Mapping the way

This is a map of my vacation.

Travel Journal

Today is _____   I am in _____

Best travel companion _____

Worst travel companion _____

Other Stuff

FUN-O-METER
Today is...

FUN ↑   NOT ↓

- words fail!
- totally AWESOME
- Cool
- Pretty FUN
- OK
- zero fun
- BIG PAIN

MOOD Check
Today I feel...

- ☐ Funny
- ☐ Funky
- ☐ Furious
- ☐ Angry
- ☐ Awesome
- ☐ Anxious
- ☐ Elated
- ☐ Eager
- ☐ Energetic
- ☐ Other

2B continued

Weather or Not
Today's weather is...

Autographs

Here's a list of autographs—including family and friends and anyone else I've met along the way.

Travel Journal

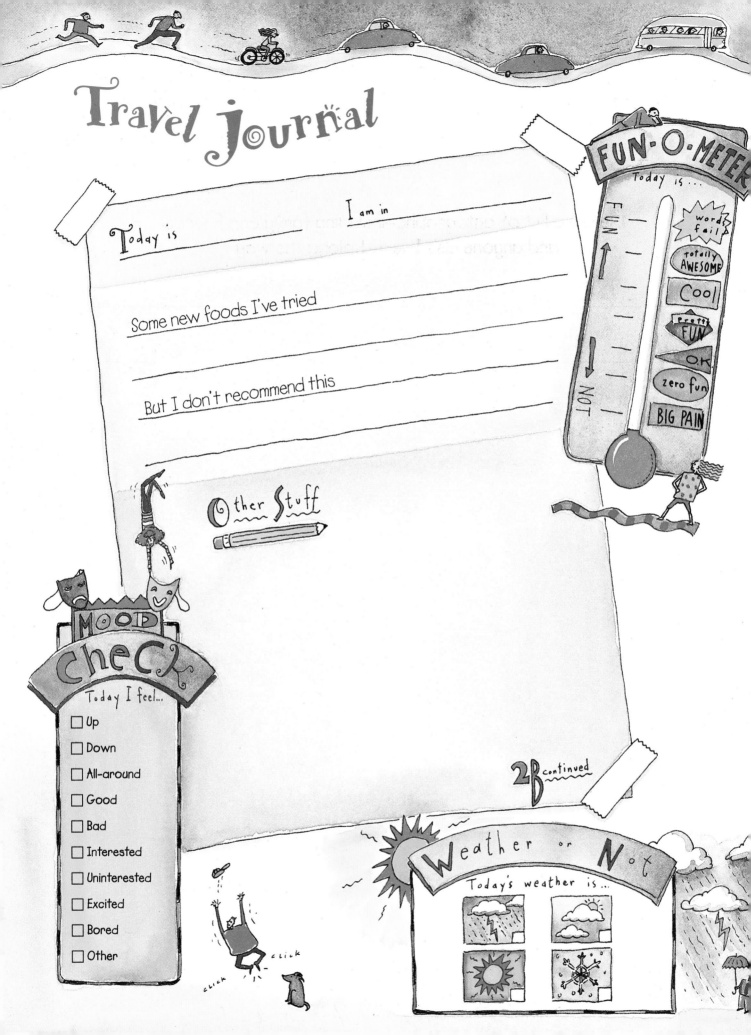

Today is _____ I am in _____

Some new foods I've tried _____

But I don't recommend this _____

Other Stuff

FUN·O·METER
Today is...

- word fail
- totally AWESOME
- Cool
- pretty FUN
- OK
- zero fun
- BIG PAIN

FUN — NOT

2B continued

MOOD CheCk
Today I feel...

- ☐ Up
- ☐ Down
- ☐ All-around
- ☐ Good
- ☐ Bad
- ☐ Interested
- ☐ Uninterested
- ☐ Excited
- ☐ Bored
- ☐ Other

Weather or Not
Today's weather is...

Memories

Saving stuff like ticket stubs, postcards, and pictures will always remind me of my trip. That's why I put them here.

Travel Journal

Today is _____ I am in _____

What I like about this place _____

_____

What I don't like _____

_____

Other Stuff

FUN-O-METER
Today is...

FUN
↑
NOT
↓

words fail
totally AWESOME
Cool
pretty FUN
O.K.
zero fun
BIG PAIN

MOOD CHECK
Today I feel...

☐ Thoughtful
☐ Carefree
☐ Careless
☐ Sporty
☐ Jolly
☐ Goofy
☐ Witty
☐ Friendly
☐ Unfriendly
☐ Other

2B continued

click click click

Weather or Not
Today's weather is...

On one side of the postcard I've drawn a picture from my trip. The other side tells all about it.

To:

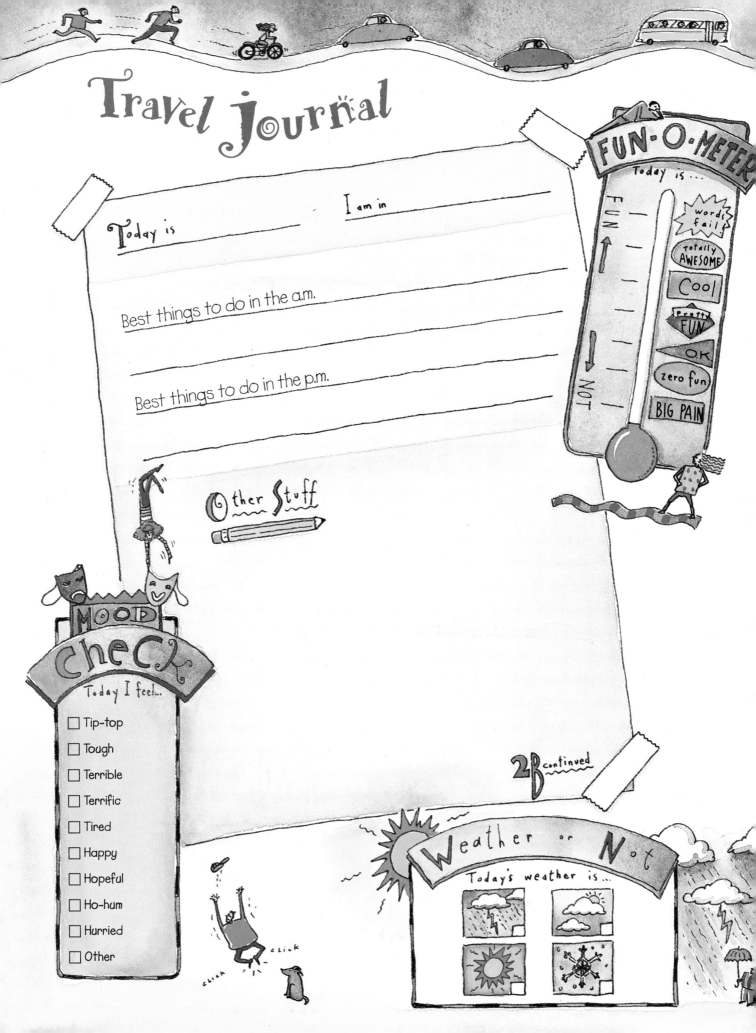

Travel Journal

Today is _____   I am in _____

Best things to do in the a.m. _____
_____

Best things to do in the p.m. _____
_____

_____

Other Stuff

FUN-O-METER
Today is...

FUN
NOT

words fail
totally AWESOME
Cool
Pretty FUN
OK
zero fun
BIG PAIN

MOOD CHECK
Today I feel...

☐ Tip-top
☐ Tough
☐ Terrible
☐ Terrific
☐ Tired
☐ Happy
☐ Hopeful
☐ Ho-hum
☐ Hurried
☐ Other

2B continued

Weather or Not
Today's weather is...

Thumbs Up / Thumbs Down

Here's the best-of-my-trip list.

Here's the worst-of-my-trip list.

Places to go

Things to do

People I've Met

Food & Restaurants

Souvenir

official movie star glasses $$

Travel Journal

Today is _____   I am in _____

Can't wait to do this _____

But I'm sick of this _____

Other Stuff

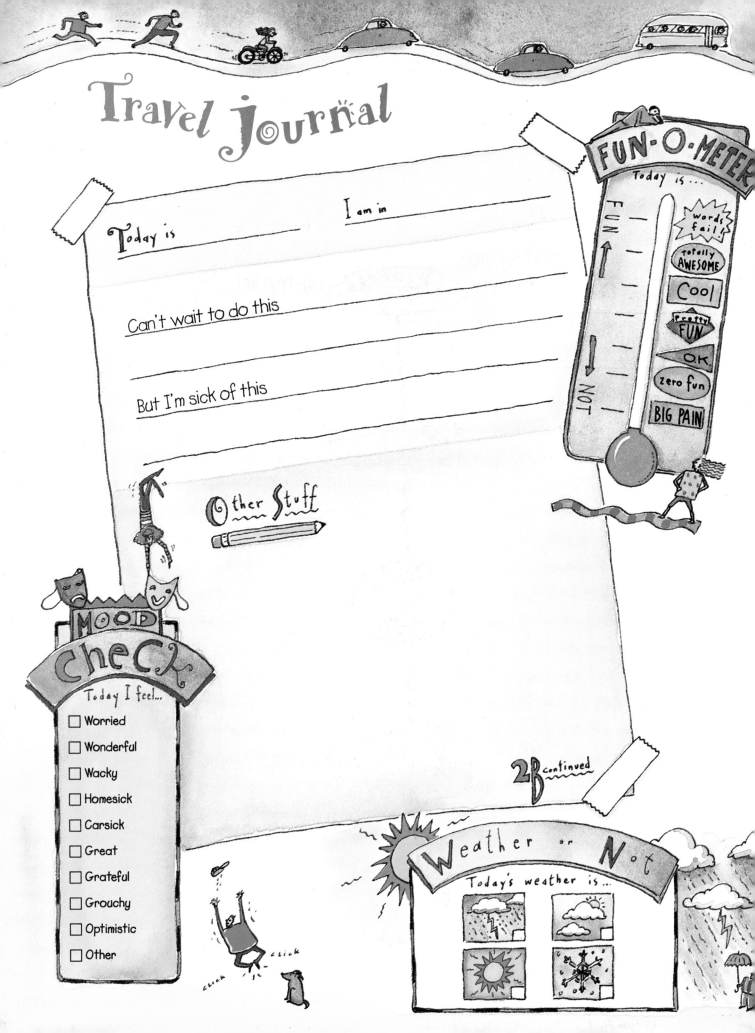

FUN-O-METER
Today is...

FUN
NOT

words fail!
totally AWESOME
Cool
Pretty FUN
O.K.
zero fun
BIG PAIN

MOOD CHECK
Today I feel...

- ☐ Worried
- ☐ Wonderful
- ☐ Wacky
- ☐ Homesick
- ☐ Carsick
- ☐ Great
- ☐ Grateful
- ☐ Grouchy
- ☐ Optimistic
- ☐ Other

2B continued

Weather or Not
Today's weather is...

Here's Me!

These pictures show how I looked at the beginning and end of the day.

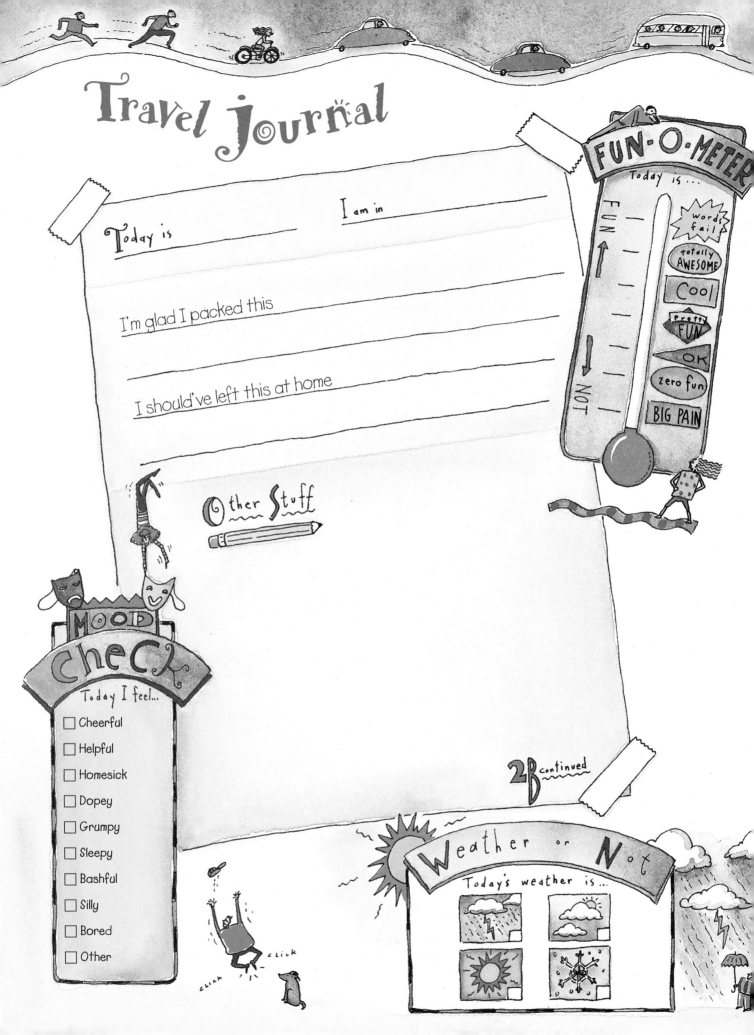

Travel Journal

Today is _____ I am in _____

I'm glad I packed this _____

I should've left this at home _____

Other Stuff

FUN-O-METER
Today is...

FUN

NOT

words fail

totally AWESOME

Cool

Pretty FUN

O.K.

zero fun

BIG PAIN

MOOD CheCK
Today I feel...

- ☐ Cheerful
- ☐ Helpful
- ☐ Homesick
- ☐ Dopey
- ☐ Grumpy
- ☐ Sleepy
- ☐ Bashful
- ☐ Silly
- ☐ Bored
- ☐ Other

2B continued

Weather or Not
Today's weather is...

On the Go!

I've checked off all the types of transportation I've tried on my trip and, just for the record, a few I'd like to try someday.

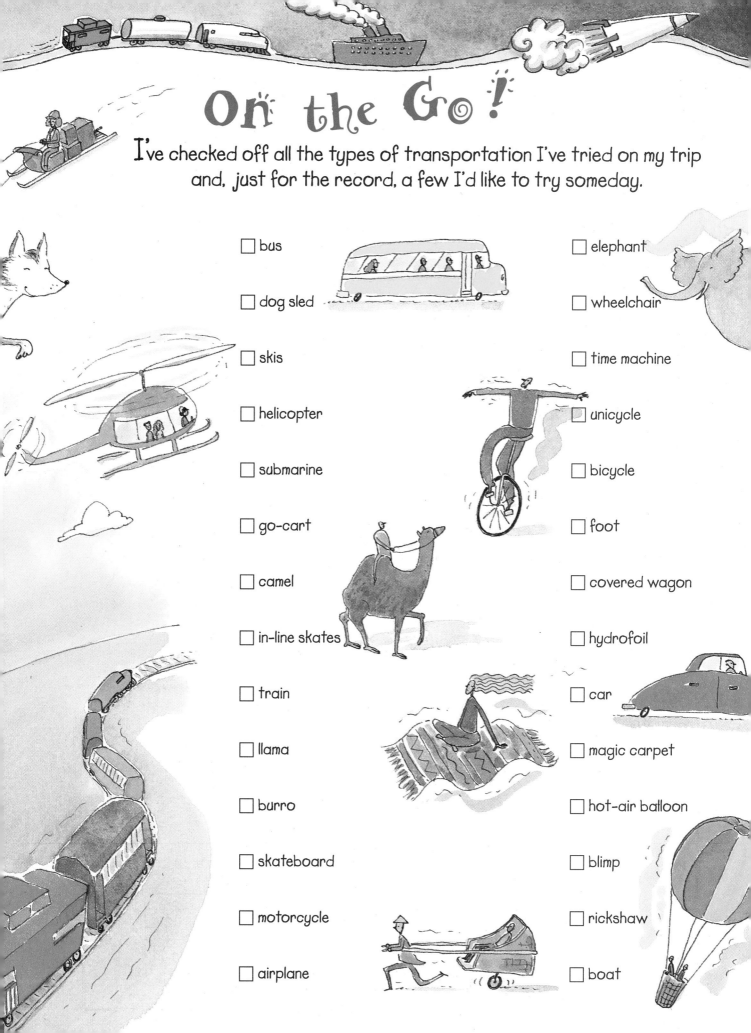

- ☐ bus
- ☐ dog sled
- ☐ skis
- ☐ helicopter
- ☐ submarine
- ☐ go-cart
- ☐ camel
- ☐ in-line skates
- ☐ train
- ☐ llama
- ☐ burro
- ☐ skateboard
- ☐ motorcycle
- ☐ airplane

- ☐ elephant
- ☐ wheelchair
- ☐ time machine
- ☐ unicycle
- ☐ bicycle
- ☐ foot
- ☐ covered wagon
- ☐ hydrofoil
- ☐ car
- ☐ magic carpet
- ☐ hot-air balloon
- ☐ blimp
- ☐ rickshaw
- ☐ boat

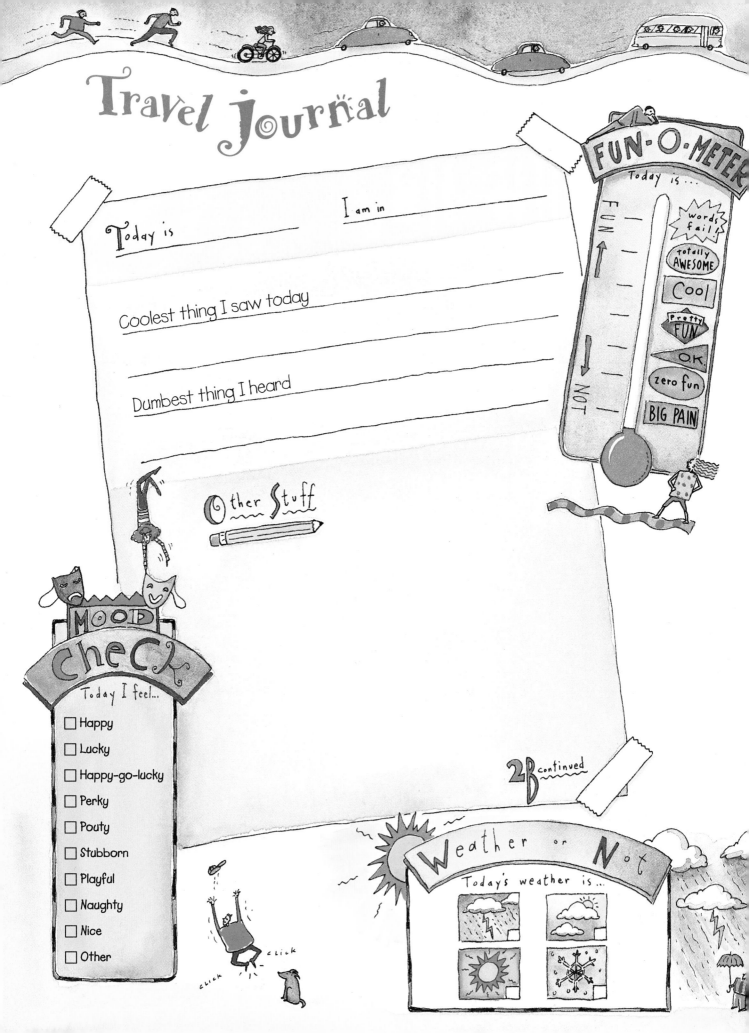

Travel Journal

Today is _____ I am in _____

Coolest thing I saw today _____

Dumbest thing I heard _____

Other Stuff

FUN-O-METER
Today is...

FUN

NOT

words fail!

totally AWESOME

Cool

Pretty FUN

O.K.

zero fun

BIG PAIN

MOOD CHECK
Today I feel...

☐ Happy
☐ Lucky
☐ Happy-go-lucky
☐ Perky
☐ Pouty
☐ Stubborn
☐ Playful
☐ Naughty
☐ Nice
☐ Other

2B continued

Weather or Not
Today's weather is...

click click click

Vacation Lingo

Brother, sister, mother, dad—please shut up you drive me MAD!
I've heard these things one too many times on this trip.

Travel Journal

Today is _____   I am in _____

I can't believe I did this _____

But this was so typical of me _____

Other Stuff

FUN-O-METER
Today is...

FUN
NOT

words fail!
totally AWESOME
Cool
Pretty FUN
O.K.
zero fun
BIG PAIN

MOOD CHECK
Today I feel...

☐ Funny
☐ Funky
☐ Furious
☐ Angry
☐ Awesome
☐ Anxious
☐ Elated
☐ Eager
☐ Energetic
☐ Other

2B continued

Weather or Not
Today's weather is...

click click click

Traveler's Herald

This was a news-making adventure I had.

★ THE ★ HERALD ★

Travel Journal

Today is _____ I am in _____

Best souvenirs so far _____

I wasted my money on this _____

_____

Other Stuff

FUN-O-METER
Today is...

FUN

NOT

- words fail!
- totally AWESOME
- Cool
- pretty FUN
- O.K.
- zero fun
- BIG PAIN

MOOD check
Today I feel...

- ☐ Up
- ☐ Down
- ☐ All-around
- ☐ Good
- ☐ Bad
- ☐ Interested
- ☐ Uninterested
- ☐ Excited
- ☐ Bored
- ☐ Other

2B continued

Weather or Not
Today's weather is...

Memories

Saving stuff like ticket stubs, postcards, and pictures will always remind me of my trip. That's why I put them here.

Travel Journal

Today is _____   I am in _____

Most awesome landmarks _____

Worst tourist traps _____

O ther Stuff

FUN-O-METER
Today is...

FUN
words fail!
totally AWESOME
COOL
pretty FUN
OK
zero fun
BIG PAIN
NOT

MOOD CHECK
Today I feel...
- ☐ Thoughtful
- ☐ Carefree
- ☐ Careless
- ☐ Sporty
- ☐ Jolly
- ☐ Goofy
- ☐ Witty
- ☐ Friendly
- ☐ Unfriendly
- ☐ Other

2B continued

Weather or Not
Today's weather is...

Travel log

Here are my "been there, done that" lists—and a few others, too.

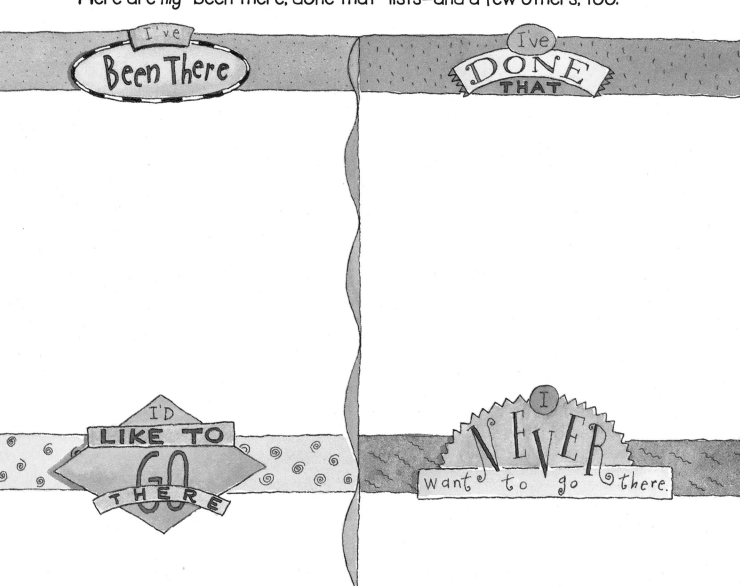

I've **Been There**

I've **DONE THAT**

I'D **LIKE TO GO THERE**

I **NEVER** want to go there.

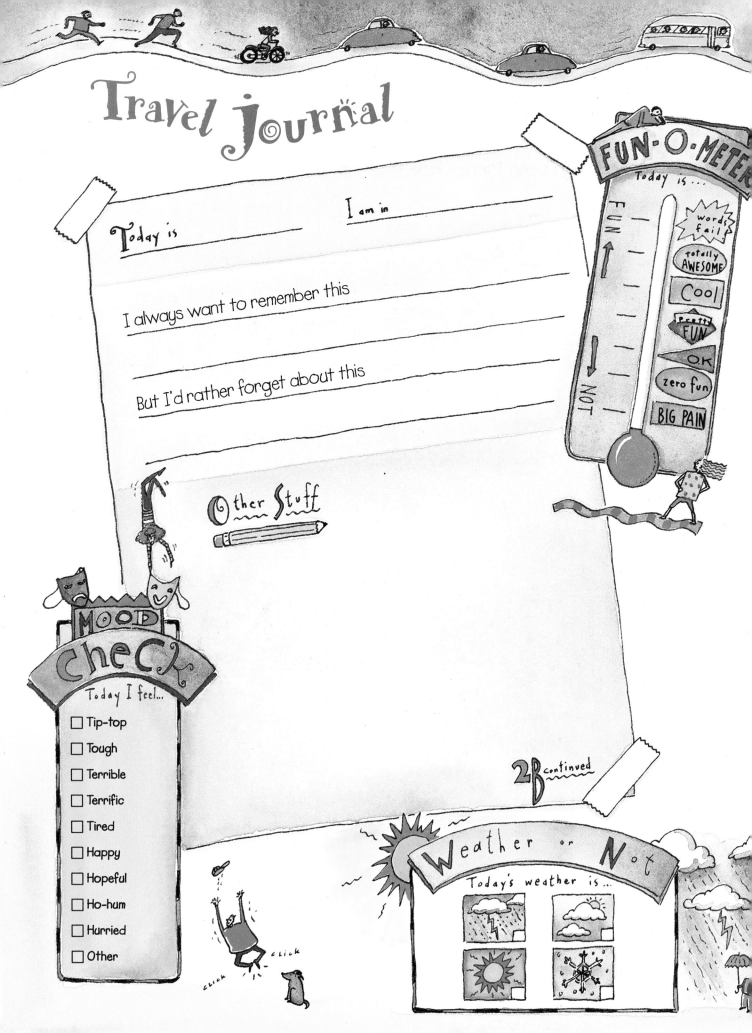

Travel Journal

Today is _____ I am in _____

I always want to remember this _____

But I'd rather forget about this _____

Other Stuff

FUN-O-METER
Today is...

FUN
NOT

words fail
totally AWESOME
Cool
pretty FUN
OK
zero fun
BIG PAIN

MOOD check
Today I feel...

☐ Tip-top
☐ Tough
☐ Terrible
☐ Terrific
☐ Tired
☐ Happy
☐ Hopeful
☐ Ho-hum
☐ Hurried
☐ Other

2B continued

click click

Weather or Not
Today's weather is...

Fantasy Vacation

Here's a picture of the best vacation I can imagine.

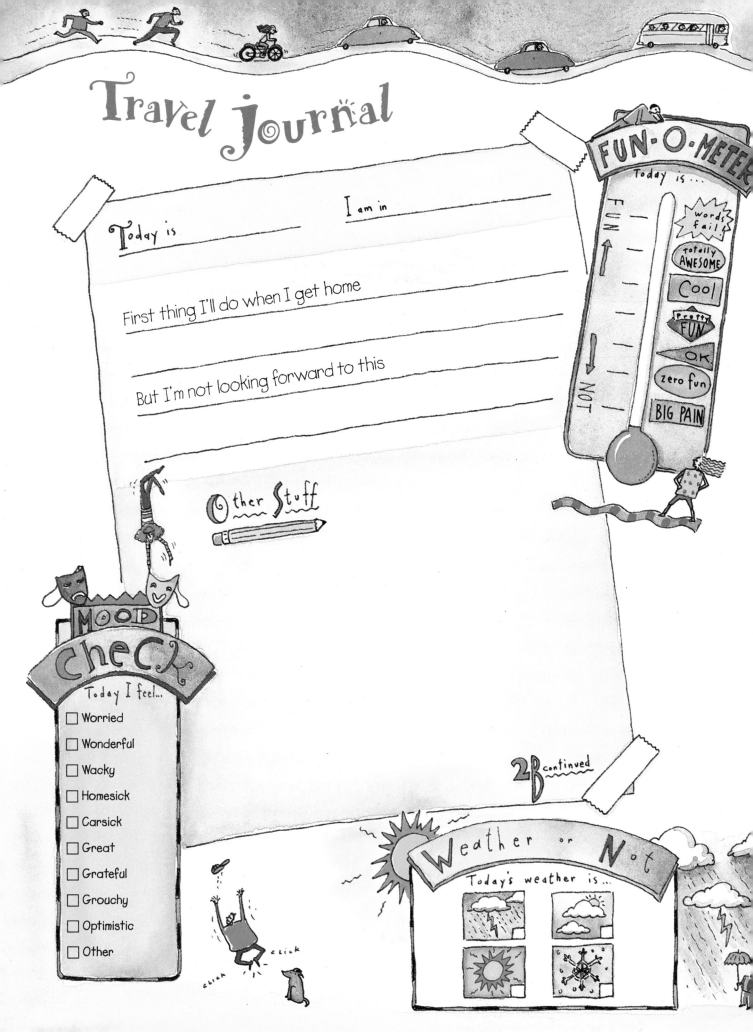

Travel Journal

Today is _____ I am in _____

First thing I'll do when I get home _____

But I'm not looking forward to this _____

Other Stuff

FUN-O-METER
Today is...

FUN
NOT

words fail!
totally AWESOME
Cool
Pretty FUN
O.K.
zero fun
BIG PAIN

MOOD check
Today I feel...

☐ Worried
☐ Wonderful
☐ Wacky
☐ Homesick
☐ Carsick
☐ Great
☐ Grateful
☐ Grouchy
☐ Optimistic
☐ Other

2B continued

Weather or Not
Today's weather is...

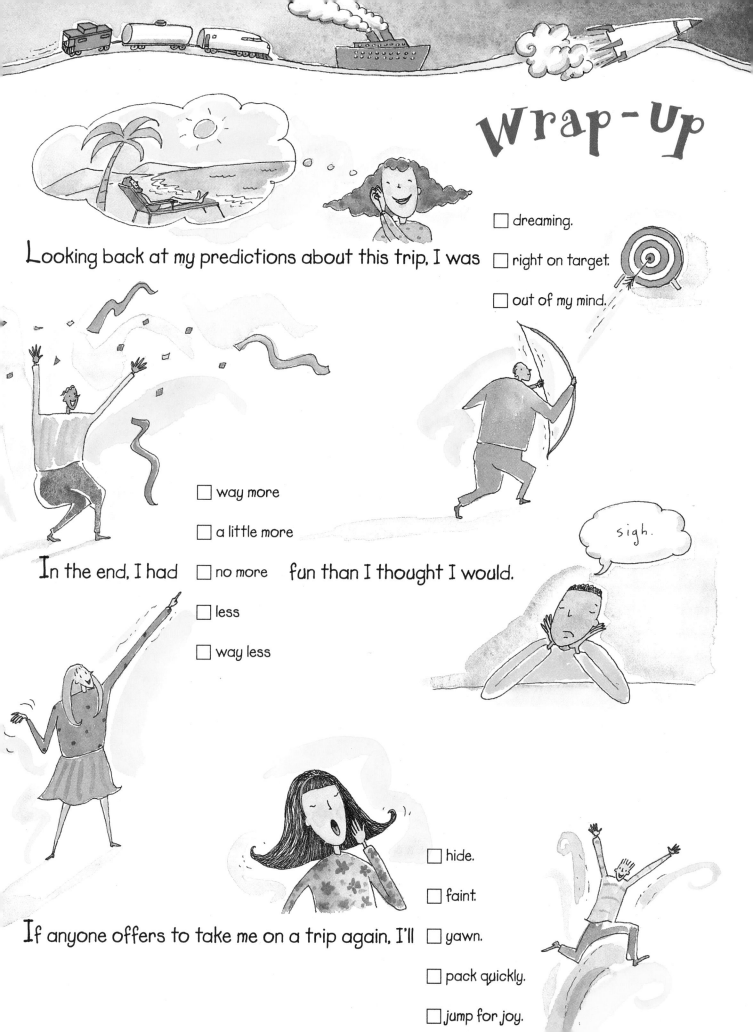

Wrap-Up

Looking back at my predictions about this trip, I was

☐ dreaming.

☐ right on target.

☐ out of my mind.

In the end, I had

☐ way more

☐ a little more

☐ no more   fun than I thought I would.

☐ less

☐ way less

sigh.

If anyone offers to take me on a trip again, I'll

☐ hide.

☐ faint.

☐ yawn.

☐ pack quickly.

☐ jump for joy.

Road-Tested

I Spy

If you are "it," choose an object, like a red button, and say: "I spy with my little eye something red." The other players then take turns trying to guess what the object is. The person who guesses the answer gets to be "it." HINT: Don't give the answer away by staring at the object.

Name That Tune

Players take turns thinking of songs and humming them for one another, a few notes at time, while the others try to be the first to "name that tune." Once you have a tune in mind, hum just the first three notes. If nobody recognizes it, hum the first four notes. Keep adding notes one at a time until someone guesses the name of the song. The first person to guess becomes the next "hummer." (Good whistlers can whistle their tunes.)

Make Me Laugh

This game is serious fun. No kidding! One person becomes the "jester" and the rest are "stonefaces." Stonefaces must never laugh or smile—if they do, their faces break. Of course the jester thinks this is funny and likes nothing more than to make stonefaces crack up. That's the game! The jester has to crack up the stonefaces. The jester can make faces, funny noises, tell jokes, but cannot tickle or touch the stonefaces to make them laugh. The last stoneface to laugh gets to be the next jester.

City Train

If you know the names of a lot of cities, take a ride on the City Train. The rules are simple—players take turns saying the names of cities. The only catch is that each city name must begin with the letter that ended the last one. For example, Houston might be followed by New York, which might be followed by Kansas City, and so on. Any player who can't come up with a city has to get off the train. The last one riding the City Train is the winner. All aboard!

Rochambeau

This game, sometimes called "Rock, Paper, Scissors," works best with two or three players. These are the rules—paper (flat hand) covers rock, rock (fist) breaks scissors, and scissors (move first two fingers like a scissors) cut paper. All players put their fists out together to the beat of Rochambeau (Ro-Sham-Bo). On "Bo," each player forms either rock, paper, or scissors. Then everybody has to follow the rules.

Travel Games

A—My Name Is . . .

Here's a "fill in the blank" game that works its way through the alphabet. It's best when the pressure of keeping the rhythm going makes players work especially hard. Here's how a boy might start things off beginning with the letter A: "A—my name is Abner, my sister's name is Anne, we come from Alaska and we sell Axes." A girl might follow, "B—my name is Bertha, my brother's name is Bert, we come from Boston and we sell Beans. You get the idea—you're out when you can't complete the sentence or when you break the tempo.

Buzz

If you've got a head for numbers, buzz is for you. First, players pick a number from 2 through 9. That number becomes *buzz*. Once *buzz* is named, players take turns counting, starting with 1. If *buzz* is 3, whenever you get to a number that contains a 3 or is a multiple of 3, you must say *buzz*. Players who mess up are out, and counting starts over again from 1. The last player remaining wins. For a challenge, play bizz-buzz, picking two numbers instead of just one. One number is *bizz*, and the other is *buzz*.

Plate-O-Grams

This game has no winners or losers—just some funny messages. To start, somebody has to spot a license plate and read the letters on the plate to everyone. For example, the letters might be "B-R-G." Next, everyone thinks of a three-word message beginning with those letters. In this case, people might come up with "Big Round Globs" or "Beware Rabid Gerbils." (You might want to allow "little" words so the plate-o-grams make more sense, for example, "My Brother is Really Gross.")

Categories

This game is good for many ages, since it can be made as easy or as difficult as you want. It all has to do with categories. One person thinks of a category—any category. It could be colors, capital cities, sports teams, or anything you can think of. Then players take turns naming items in the category. The game ends when someone repeats something already mentioned or when players can't think of any other items in the category.

Alphabet Derby

This is a race to the end of the alphabet. To play, you must find all the letters of the alphabet—in order. Letters may be found on road signs, billboards, bumper stickers, license plates, etc. You don't have to announce each letter you find, but if asked, you must tell what letter you are on. If challenged, you should be able to say where you saw your letters. The first one to Z wins. (To make things go more quickly, you may want to agree that Q is the only letter that can be found out of order.)

20 Questions

This old standby is simple, but fun. One player thinks of something (anything you can see, smell, hear, or touch) and tells the others if it is animal, vegetable, or mineral. The others take turns asking "yes-or-no" questions to try to figure out what it is. At any time a player may use a turn to guess what it is. It's best to ask a lot of questions before you start guessing, but remember, you only have twenty questions. Whoever guesses right wins. You can play this game using other categories, too, like famous people, places, or whatever—be creative!

The Twelve Days of Our Trip
(to the tune of "The Twelve Days of Christmas")

On the first day of our trip this is what I saw—
the baby throw up in the car.

On the second day of our trip this is what I saw—
two pick-up trucks and the baby throw up in the car.

Third day:
Fourth day:
Fifth day:
Sixth day:
Seventh day:
Eighth day:
Ninth day:
Tenth day:
Eleventh day:
Twelfth day:

three dead skunks
four minivans
five backseat fights
six broken headlights
seven miles of road work
eight cars a-speeding
nine railroad crossings
ten roadside rest stops
eleven cop cars hiding
twelve bumper stickers

Songs to drive

Your Destination! 99 mi.

Backseat Border Blues
(to the tune of "This Land is Your Land")

This side is my side; that side is your side.
Let's get along now; this is a long ride.
You see this line here—please don't cross over.
One side for you and one for me.

I had my eyes closed—faked I was sleeping.
So you got greedy and started creeping.
Try that again, Bub, and you'll be weeping.
One side for you and one for me.

Just like I warned you—now you are crying.
And Dad is angry—now you are lying.
You had it coming, there's no denying.
One side for you and one for me.

99 Miles to Go on Our Trip
(to the tune of "99 Bottles")

99 miles to go on our trip.
99 miles to go.
Step on the gas. I think we can pass.
98 miles to go on our trip. . .

(Keep repeating until you get to
"0 miles to go" or until someone
kicks you out of the car, whichever
comes first.)

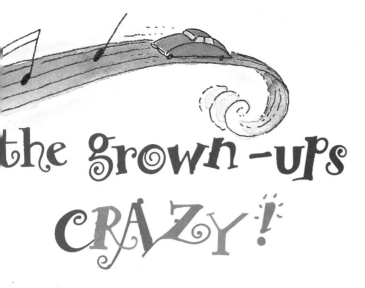

the grown-ups CRAZY!

Are We Lost?
(to the tune of "Are You Sleeping?")

Are we lost? Are we lost?
Yes we are. Yes we are.
Someone get a map out. Someone get a map out.
Find the way. Find the way.

(Save this one for when you *really* get lost. Sing it as a round—as you drive around and around—and you're sure to drive the grown-ups crazy.)

Don't Get Out of the Fast Lane
(to the tune of "Take Me out to the Ball Game")

Don't get out of the fast lane.
Don't let up on the gas.
I can't believe all the cars we've passed—
Wherever we're going, we're going there fast.
And its zoom, zoom, zoom down the freeway,
But don't break the speed limit please.
Or the friend-ly Highway Patrol
Will request your keys!

Battle Hymn of the Brat
(to the tune of "Battle Hymn of the Republic")

Our minivan is loaded to the roof with games and toys.
We've all had snacks and found a station everyone enjoys.
The kids are all behaving well; we've hardly made a noise.
But something's not quite right.

(Chorus)
I'M NOT HAVING ANY FUN YET.
I'M NOT HAVING ANY FUN YET.
I'M NOT HAVING ANY FUN YET.
THIS TRIP IS DRAGGING ON.

We've hit every tourist trap from Maine to Monterey,
Miami to Mount Rushmore, Plymouth Rock to Frisco Bay.
We wait in never-ending lines forever and a day.
It's time to take a rest.

(Chorus)

Now you might think that I'm spoiled, that my attitude is bad.
You wouldn't be the first if my complaining makes you mad.
In fact you'd be the third, behind my Mother and my Dad.
But I still feel like this:

(Chorus)

When-You-Get-There

Paper Airplane Games

Find some paper and follow the paper airplane instructions. Then you can play games with your paper planes. 1) Go for distance. Whose plane can fly the farthest? 2) Fly for accuracy. Who can land closest to a chosen target? 3) Stay aloft. Whose plane can stay in the air the longest?

Fold, then unfold on ①

Fold down corners
Fold down on line ②

Fold down corners again

Fold little flap up

Fold this side back to meet other side

Fold wings down on both sides

Hide the Doohickey

Any small object will do in this game that is fun for kids of all ages. One player hides the object while the others wait in another room. Players are then called back to find the object. Younger players might need to be told if they are "warm" or "cold." The first player to find the object gets to hide it next.

Bright Ideas

If you have a flashlight you will never be bored again, at least not until you wear the battery out. Set up a flashlight in a dark room and make hand shadow figures on the wall. Tell a scary story while projecting a spider or a ghost onto the ceiling. Cut out shadow puppets and put on a show. With more than one flashlight, you can play flashlight tag after dark—instead of tagging people, you hit them with your beam of light. A flashlight can also add a scary touch to face-making. Turn out the lights and see how scary you can look!

Learn to Girn

Face facts, faces are funny. Take your face to a mirror and see just how funny it can get. Serious face-makers call it "girning." It's even funnier if you have someone else to girn with. Work on blinks, winks, sneers, grimaces, grins, eyebrow raises, sidelong glances, or whatever. How many emotions can you show? How many faces can you make?

Games

Wastebasket H-O-R-S-E

A wastebasket makes a good indoor basketball hoop, and horse is a good indoor game. In horse, players take turns shooting for the hoop from various places on the court. Use rolled-up socks, crumpled-up paper or an appropriate indoor ball. If a player makes a shot, the next player must make it, too. One miss, and you get an H; two misses, an H-O; and so on. Miss five times and you are out with H-O-R-S-E.

Sock Soccer

This game is just like it sounds. Roll up some socks, set up some goals, agree on a rule or two, and start kicking. (WARNING: According to the American Sock Soccer Association, using lamps and plants for goalposts can get you in an awful lot of trouble!)

Slo-mo Volleyball

If you have any balloons left over from the water balloon toss, fill one with air for this slow motion, indoor version of volleyball. Play on your knees using a bed, couch, or some chairs for a net. You give up a point when you hit the balloon out, let it touch the ground, or fail to get it over in the agreed upon number of hits. Spike it, Dude, but don't let it pop!

Water Balloon Toss

In this damp contest, players pair up and form two lines facing each other. Each pair gets a balloon. One at a time, one person in each pair tosses the balloon to the other. After each successful toss, the tosser backs up a full step. The pair completing the longest toss wins and gets to stay dry! Most grown-ups will insist that you play this game outside.

Whirly-Bird

Make a simple paper helicopter using the instructions. Decorate your whirly-bird with markers or crayons before you cut it out. Drop your whirly-bird from a high place. When the wind is right, your whirly-bird will stay in the air for a long time. Watch it land, and then be sure to get it and fly it again.

Cut at ①, ②, ③

Fold:
Ⓐ Back
Ⓑ Forward
Ⓒ As shown

Fold up

Knot Fun!

Grab some lanyard—you know, that brightly-colored plastic lacing. Then get busy making knots to create friendship bracelets, book marks, key chains, or anything else you can think of.

If you're making a bracelet, the quick knot and diamond knot work great because you start out with a loop. When you finish, tie the loose ends in an overhand knot that can slip through the loop to close the bracelet.

To make a key chain, start by attaching your lanyard to a key hook or ring. Then start knotting!

The Quick Knot

1. Cut one color of lanyard about 2 feet long. Cut another color about 3 feet long. Fold the shorter strand in half and tie it together with the longer strand, making sure you have a loop above the knot (see illustration). Hang the loop on something steady so you can use both hands to work.

2. Arrange the strands as shown in the illustration. The longer strand (A) will wrap around the shorter strands (B and C). First, cross strand A <u>over</u> strand B and <u>under</u> strand C. Then pull up on strand A so it's tight and close to the starter knot.

3. Next, cross strand A <u>over</u> strand C and <u>under</u> strand B. Then pull strand A tight again.

4. Keep going back and forth following steps 2 and 3 until you're finished.

The Box Knot

1. Start with two colors of lanyard. Cut a piece from each color exactly the same length. You'll need a lot of lanyard for this knot, so figure on using strands that are at least 4-feet long, depending on what you're making. Put the two pieces together, making a regular overhand knot in the center. Spread out the strands so one color is in a line going up and down and the other color in a line going left and right. You now have four strands (A, B, C, and D).

2. To begin the box knot, cross strand A right and strand C left leaving loops you can weave under and over as shown in the illustration.

3. Next, bring strand B down, crossing <u>over</u> strand C and <u>under</u> strand A.

4. Then, bring strand D up, crossing <u>over</u> strand A and <u>under</u> strand C. Now pull on all the strands to tighten the knot. Continue following steps 2-4 to make more box knots.

The Diamond Knot

1. Grab two different colors of lanyard, each about 3 feet long. Fold each strand in half and tie the strands together at the top, making sure you have a loop above the knot (see illustration). Now you have four strands of equal length. Keep two strands of one color on the right and two strands of the other color on the left. Hang the loop on something steady so you can use both hands to work.

2. Cross strand D <u>under</u> strands C and B and <u>over</u> strand B as shown in the illustration.

3. Next, cross strand A <u>under</u> strands B and D and <u>over</u> strand D. (This is kind of tricky, but don't give up—keep practicing.) Then, pull up tightly so the diamond knot is close to the starter knot.

4. Start your next knot and keep following steps 2 and 3 until your creation is just the right length.

Don't miss your flight!

Hurry and find your seat before the plane takes off!

Travel ⏲ time

Where are these travelers going?
Match the people waiting in the ticket line with their destination. Use the objects that the people are carrying and their clothing as clues.

1___
2___
3___
4___
5___
6___
7___
8___
9___

TICKETS

DESTINATIONS

A

B

C

D

E

F

G

H

I

Picture Park

Can you find 22 words hidden in the tree? Look across, up, down, backwards, and diagonally. All the words listed below are pictured on this page.

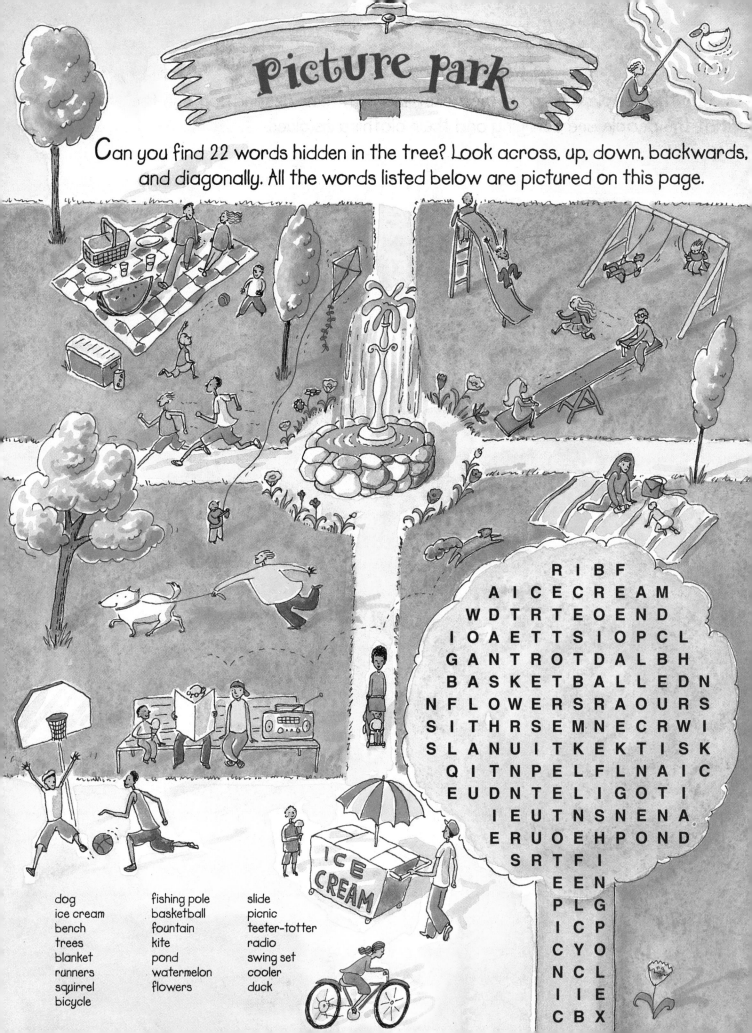

Word list:

- dog
- ice cream
- bench
- trees
- blanket
- runners
- squirrel
- bicycle
- fishing pole
- basketball
- fountain
- kite
- pond
- watermelon
- flowers
- slide
- picnic
- teeter-totter
- radio
- swing set
- cooler
- duck

Word search grid:

```
        R I B F
    A I C E C R E A M
    W D T R T E O E N D
  I O A E T T S I O P C L
  G A N T R O T D A L B H
  B A S K E T B A L L E D N
  N F L O W E R S R A O U R S
  S I T H R S E M N E C R W I
  S L A N U I T K E K T I S K
  Q I T N P E L F L N A I C
  E U D N T E L I G O T I
    I E U T N S N E N A
    E R U O E H P O N D
    S R T F     I
    E E     N
    P L     G
    I C     P
    I Y     O
    C C     L
    N L     E
    I I
    C B
    C X
```

The bugs at your picnic have a message for you. Use the key to fill in the blanks.

D R O P S O M E

C R U M B S

F O R U S !

key

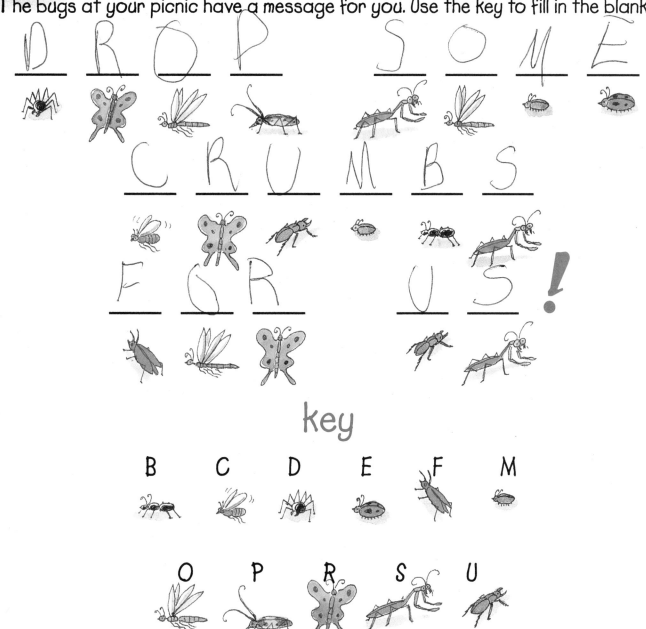

B C D E F M

O P R S U

Summer Vacation Crossword Puzzle

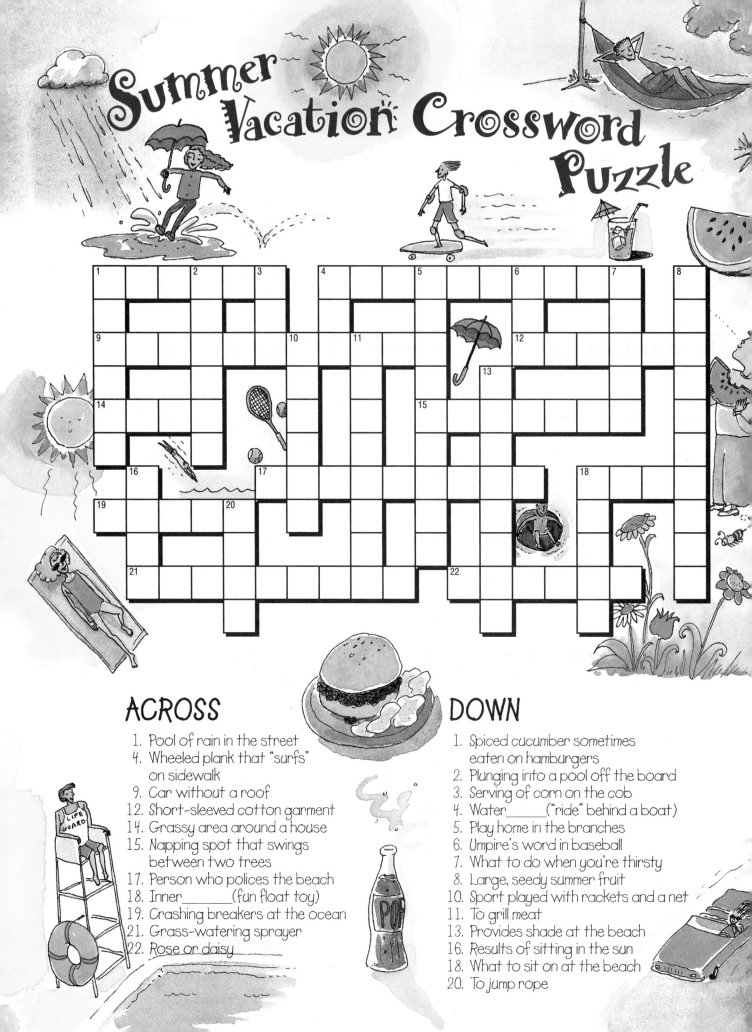

ACROSS

1. Pool of rain in the street
4. Wheeled plank that "surfs" on sidewalk
9. Car without a roof
12. Short-sleeved cotton garment
14. Grassy area around a house
15. Napping spot that swings between two trees
17. Person who polices the beach
18. Inner_____ (fun float toy)
19. Crashing breakers at the ocean
21. Grass-watering sprayer
22. Rose or daisy _____

DOWN

1. Spiced cucumber sometimes eaten on hamburgers
2. Plunging into a pool off the board
3. Serving of corn on the cob
4. Water_____ ("ride" behind a boat)
5. Play home in the branches
6. Umpire's word in baseball
7. What to do when you're thirsty
8. Large, seedy summer fruit
10. Sport played with rackets and a net
11. To grill meat
13. Provides shade at the beach
16. Results of sitting in the sun
18. What to sit on at the beach
20. To jump rope

Headline Adventure

Create your own wacky news story.
Ask somebody for words to fill in the blanks below. Then read the story aloud.

It was a _bright orange_ night and the _Jenna_ family was driving down the highway on their
      ADJECTIVE (describing word)   NAME

way to _Bickford's_. All of a sudden, they saw _101_ _police_ along the side of the
        PLACE   NUMBER   PLURAL NOUN

highway. They decided to _jump rope_ because it seemed like the right thing to do.
                          VERB

Denny's decided to call for a little _store_ and everyone else started _running_.
  NAME   NOUN   -ING WORD

When the _mountain_ arrived, everything was under control. A passerby said, "It certainly was lucky
          NOUN

that this _big_ family was driving by. Those kids knew exactly what to do
          ADJECTIVE (describing word)

in a _cloud_ like this. The kids admitted, "We were _moist_, and it was a great adventure,
      NOUN   ADJECTIVE (describing word)

but now we have to get _driving_."
                        -ING WORD

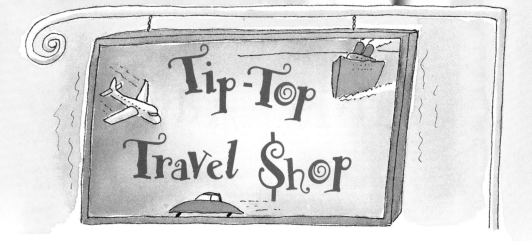

Can you find 30 things in this scene that start with the letter T?
Finding 15 is tricky, 20 is terrific, and 25 or more is tip-top.

Make me a map

The mapmaker has fallen asleep on the job. She drew 15 states but forgot to label them. Can you match the states with their names?

1. Florida _____

2. Michigan _____

3. Oklahoma _____

4. Ohio _____

5. Louisiana _____

6. California _____

7. Hawaii _____

8. Nevada _____

9. Virginia _____

10. Tennessee _____

11. Washington _____

12. New York _____

13. Utah _____

14. Massachusetts _____

15. Idaho _____

A

B

C

D

E

F

G

H

I

J

K

L

M

N

O

This car needs a tune up. Can you unscramble the 14 parts listed below?

1. STRINGEE LEWEH _____

2. HODO _____

3. LACEORCRATE _____

4. KNURT _____

5. SWINDLEHID _____

6. BAKER _____

7. BRASHADDO _____

8. HEWEL _____

9. RIGHTSAFE _____

10. GENNIE _____

11. LADHEIGHT _____

12. BURPEM _____

13. ELFMURF _____

14. TYRETAB _____

Something's Fishy

Can you spot 10 differences between the top and bottom fish tanks?

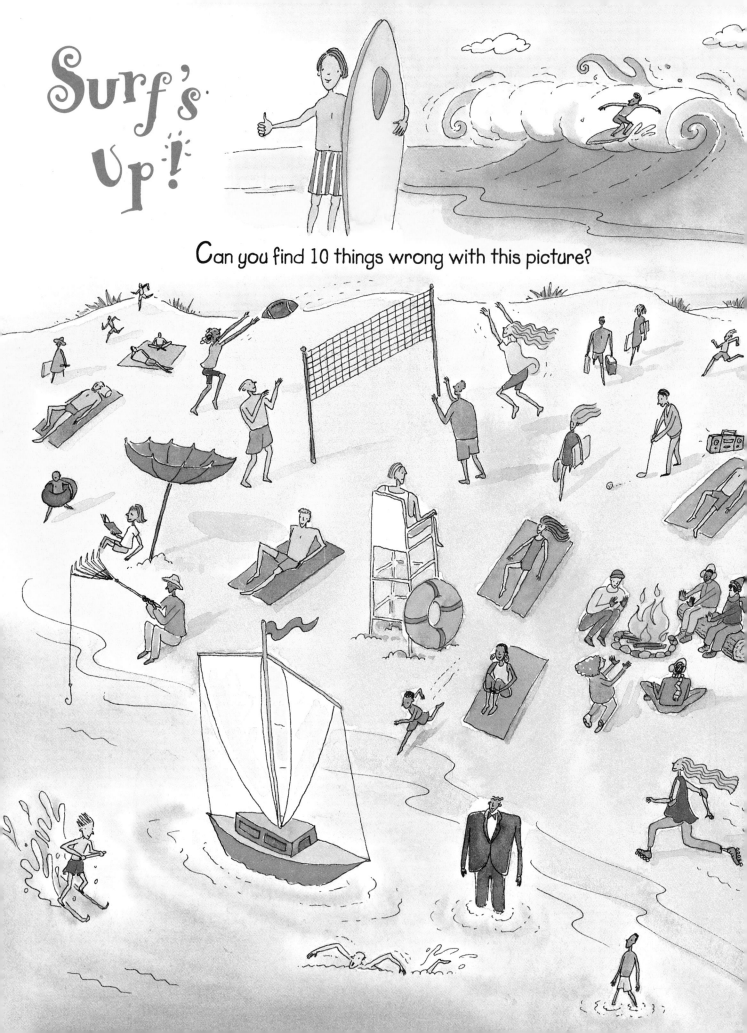

Surf's Up!

Can you find 10 things wrong with this picture?

Backseat Bingo

binjo!

This game can be played with up to four people. Select a bingo card. Each time you see one of the items pictured on the card, draw an X on that square. The first person to cross out five squares across, down, or diagonally wins.

Wacky Water Park

Call the lifeguard! There's a whale in the swimming pool. That's not the only thing wrong at this water park. Look at the picture to find 11 other strange things.

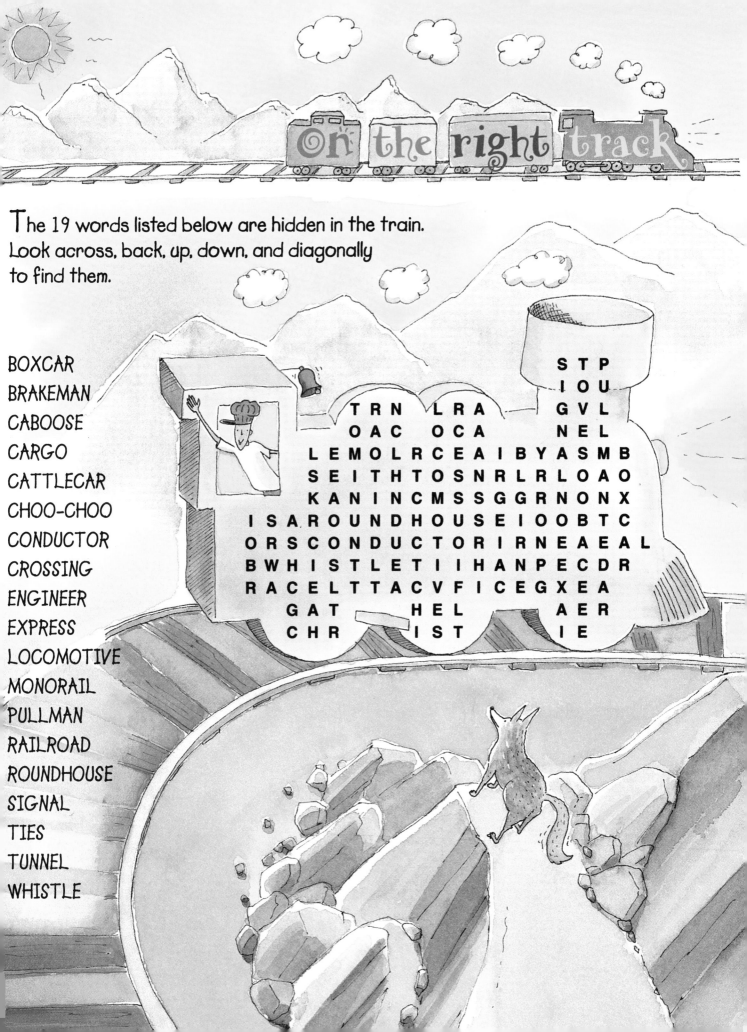

On the right track

The 19 words listed below are hidden in the train. Look across, back, up, down, and diagonally to find them.

BOXCAR
BRAKEMAN
CABOOSE
CARGO
CATTLECAR
CHOO-CHOO
CONDUCTOR
CROSSING
ENGINEER
EXPRESS
LOCOMOTIVE
MONORAIL
PULLMAN
RAILROAD
ROUNDHOUSE
SIGNAL
TIES
TUNNEL
WHISTLE

```
              T R N       L R A         S T P
              O A C       O C A         I O U
      L E M O L R C E A I B Y A S M B  G V L
      S E I T H T O S N R L R L O A O  N E L
      K A N I N C M S S G G R N O N X  E L L
    I S A R O U N D H O U S E I O O B T C
    O R S C O N D U C T O R I R N E A E A L
    B W H I S T L E T I I H A N P E C D R
    R A C E L T T A C V F I C E G X E A
      G A T       H E L         A E R
      C H R       I S T         I E
```

bloomers

How many flowers can you name using the word pictures below?

1. [butter on plate] + [cup] =

2. [pans] + **E** =

3. [snapping fingers] + [dragon] =

4. [car] + [map of USA] =

5. [fox] + [glove] =

6. [calendar] + **e** =

7. [cows] + [lips] =

8. [gold bar 24K] + **N** + [fishing pole] =

Pathways

Juan wants to go fishing, Michelle wants to do some bird watching, and Keisha wants to go rock climbing. Which trail should each person take?

Juan

Michelle

Keisha

Winter Vacation Crossword Puzzle

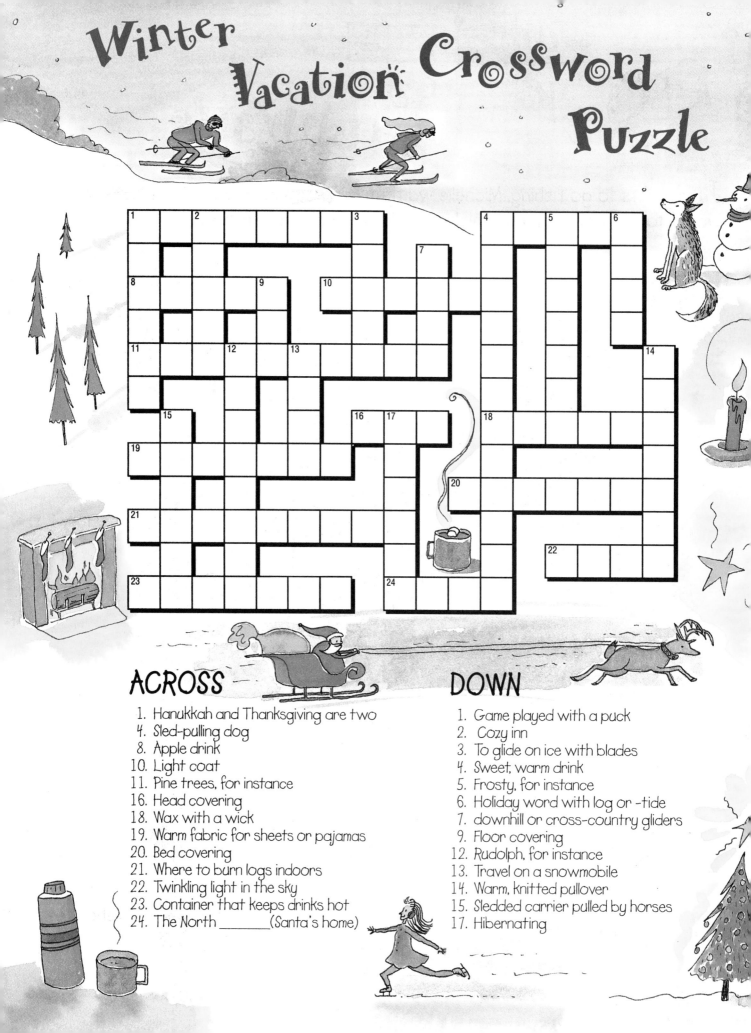

ACROSS

1. Hanukkah and Thanksgiving are two
4. Sled-pulling dog
8. Apple drink
10. Light coat
11. Pine trees, for instance
16. Head covering
18. Wax with a wick
19. Warm fabric for sheets or pajamas
20. Bed covering
21. Where to burn logs indoors
22. Twinkling light in the sky
23. Container that keeps drinks hot
24. The North _____ (Santa's home)

DOWN

1. Game played with a puck
2. Cozy inn
3. To glide on ice with blades
4. Sweet, warm drink
5. Frosty, for instance
6. Holiday word with log or -tide
7. downhill or cross-country gliders
9. Floor covering
12. Rudolph, for instance
13. Travel on a snowmobile
14. Warm, knitted pullover
15. Sledded carrier pulled by horses
17. Hibernating

Highway Robbery

It was late in the afternoon as we sped along the dusty road in the family station wagon. We were on our way to Florida for our annual family vacation and my little sister Louise was really starting to get on my nerves. We were nearly to Chattanooga when the station wagon slowed down.

"What's going on?" my mother asked.

Through the windshield I could see some sort of road-block. We slowly crept along until we reached several police officers standing by orange cones that blocked the road. An old blue convertible had been directed over to the side of the road and one of the officers was talking with the man who owned it.

My dad rolled down his window as another police officer approached our car.

"There's been a robbery at the local grocery store ten miles away," the officer explained. "We're checking cars because we think the robber is trying to get out of town."

We all got out of the car. I sat on the bumper, listening to the conversation between the other policeman and the man in the blue convertible. I noticed that his backseat was filled with grocery bags.

"Officer, I tell you, these are my things I bought a day ago in Salt Lake City," the man said. "I've been driving for 12 hours straight. I haven't even heard of the grocery store you're talking about."

The policeman looked skeptical. He strolled to the front of the car, took out a notepad, and began writing down the license plate number on the convertible.

The man was not telling the truth. Do you know what gave him away?

Happy Camper?

Help make this hungry camper a happy camper. Find the hidden fork, plate, cup, cooler, sandwich, apple, bottle of juice, and slice of cake.

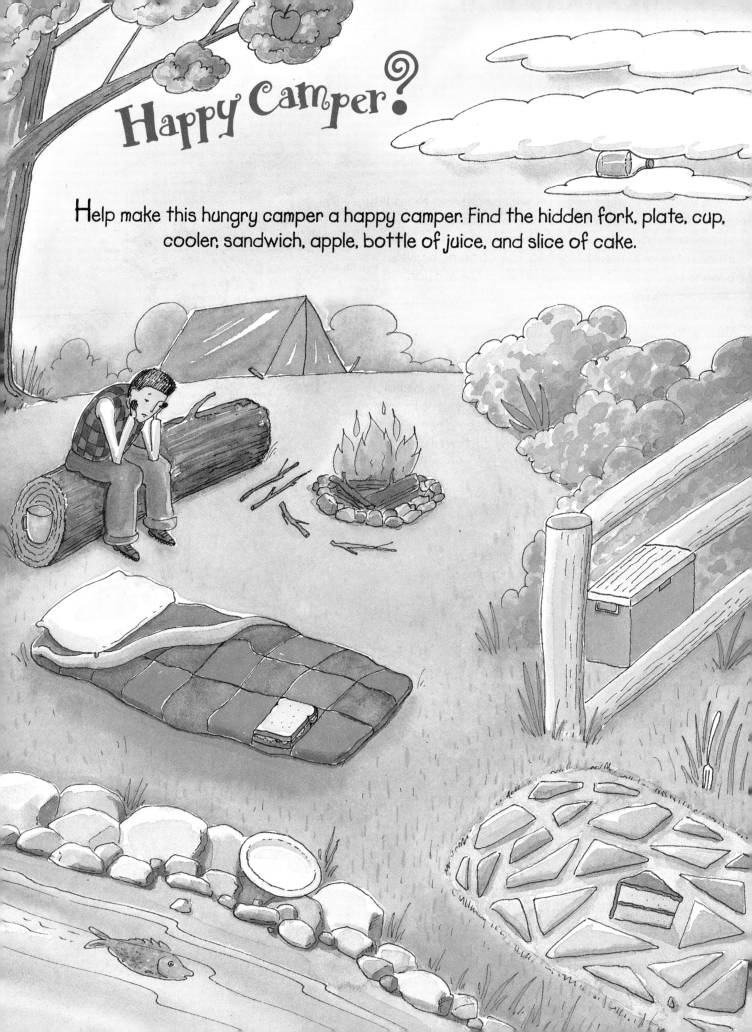

Best vacation ever!

Create your own crazy story. Ask somebody for words to fill in the blanks below. Then read the story aloud.

_____ says that the best vacation ever is a _____ trip to _____.
PERSON'S NAME   NOUN   PLACE

Once you're there, you just have to _____. And don't forget to _____. The most exciting
       VERB   VERB

things to do are _____ and _____, but only if you're wearing _____.
    ACTIVITY   ACTIVITY   TYPE OF CLOTHING

There's _____ food to eat, too. Order the _____ and _____ special
    ADJECTIVE (describing word)   NOUN   NOUN

for a real treat, and tell them _____ sent you. Before you head home, be sure to buy
       PERSON'S NAME

a _____ at the souvenir shop! It will always remind you of your _____ trip.
   NOUN   ADJECTIVE (describing word)

Your friends have left you a note on the beach. Use the key to fill in the blanks.

key

A B E F H I L M O R S T Y

Barnyard Scramble

How many of the 14 animal names can you unscramble?
All of the animals are pictured on this page.

1. GDO _____

2. ACT _____

3. OWC _____

4. ADOT _____

5. KUCD _____

6. TOGA _____

7. ORCW _____

8. OGSOE _____

9. EOMUS _____

10. SHOER _____

11. NOBRI _____

12. BRITAB _____

13. NARCOCO _____

14. RLIQEUSR _____

Souvenir

dot-to-dot

Mom brought home a souvenir from her trip to New York City.
Connect the dots in order from 1 to 71 to find out what it is.

Wait for me!

Your friends have run off to their favorite rides at the amusement park.
Use the nine squares below as hints to help you find your friends.

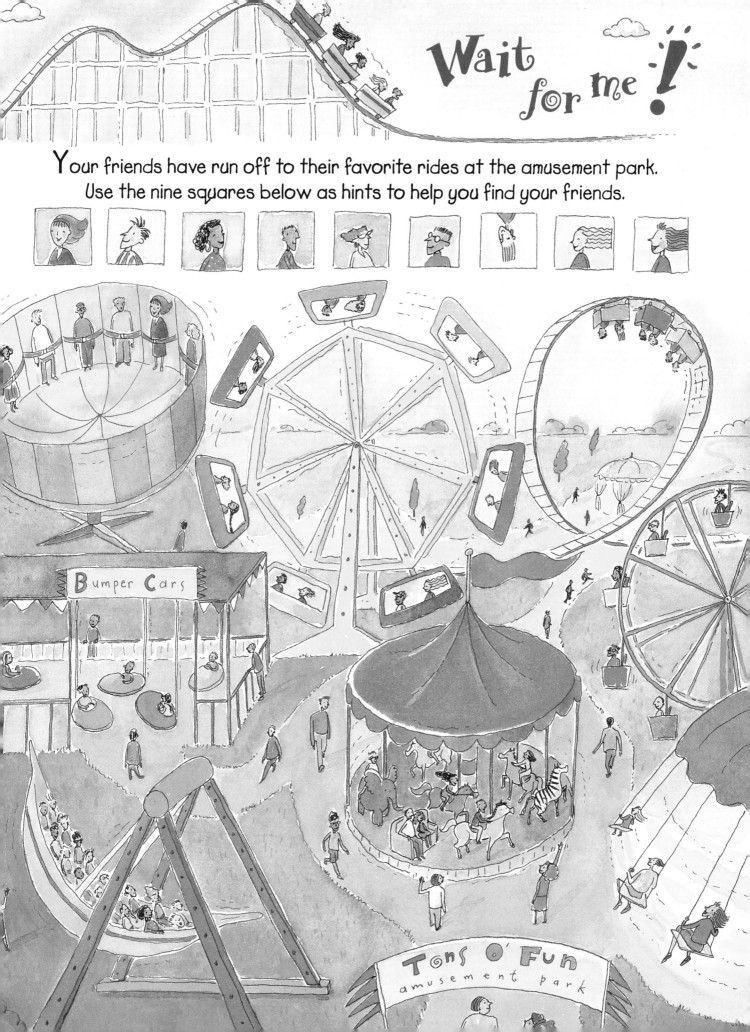

Bumper Cars

Tons O' Fun
amusement park

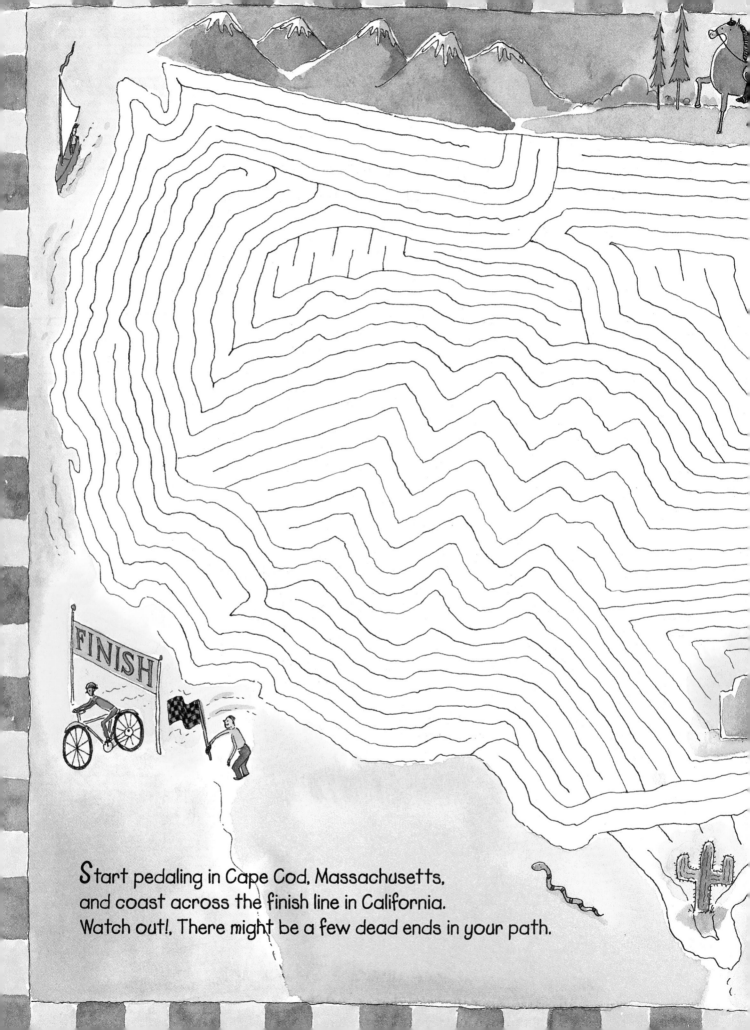

Start pedaling in Cape Cod, Massachusetts, and coast across the finish line in California. Watch out!, There might be a few dead ends in your path.

The race is On!

Start

Movie Set Match-up

There has been a mix-up on the movie set. See if you can help by matching the actors with their vehicles. Use the objects that the actors are carrying and their clothes as clues.

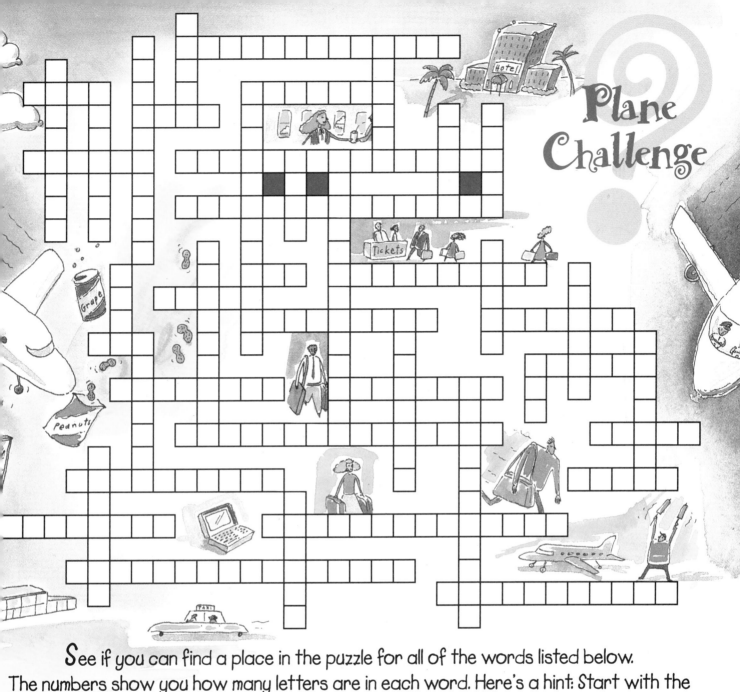

Plane Challenge

See if you can find a place in the puzzle for all of the words listed below. The numbers show you how many letters are in each word. Here's a hint: Start with the words that have 12, 14, or 16 letters in them. (Spaces between words don't count!)

3
hub
nap
sky

4
gate
ramp
soda
tags

5
aisle
coach
hotel
novel
pilot
seats
snack

6
laptop
pillow
on time
snooze
ticket

7
airport
blanket
co-pilot
deplane
parking
peanuts

8
airspeed
landings
navigate
schedule
takeoffs

9
concourse
passenger

10
first class
flight plan
turbulence

11
folding tray
landing gear

12
baggage check

13
inflight movie
ticket counter

14
carry-on luggage

15
baggage carousel
crossword puzzle
flight attendant

16
cruising altitude

Bicycle Mix-up

Looks like a bicycle mix-up. Can you find 10 other things wrong with this picture?

You have exactly 205 tickets to spend on prizes. If you want to spend exactly all of your tickets and you don't want to buy more than one of anything, which items should you buy?

Which hotel?

It's getting late and the Tyred family needs to find their hotel. They know it's on Yawn Avenue, but which hotel is it? Mr. Tyred stayed here years ago and remembers the facts below. Use them to figure out where the family should check in before everyone falls asleep!

FACTS:

1. The hotel has a circular driveway.
2. The number on the hotel is even.
3. The hotel is between two hotels that have palm trees in front of them.
4. The name of the hotel (without the word "inn" or "hotel") spells another word when it is written backwards.

Answers

Don't miss your flight!

Travel time
1. C; 2. A; 3. H; 4. F; 5. B;
6. D; 7. E; 8. G; 9. I

Picture park

You're bugging me!
"Drop some crumbs for us!"

Summer Vacation Crossword Puzzle

Tip-Top Travel Shop
There are 30 things that begin with T: table, tablecloth, tackle box, tag, tapes, taxi, teapot, teddy bear, teeth, telephone, ten (on a price tag), tennis racket, tent, thermometer, thermos, thumb, tickets, tie, tools, toothbrush, towel, toys, trees, tricycle, trunk, T-shirt, Tuesday (on calendar), turtleneck, tuxedo, and typewriter.

Make me a map
1. B; 2. J; 3. D; 4. K; 5. M; 6. E; 7. G; 8. O; 9. C; 10. A; 11. H; 12. F; 13. I; 14. L; 15. N

Auto Repair
1. steering wheel; 2. hood; 3. accelerator; 4. trunk; 5. windshield; 6. brake; 7. dashboard; 8. wheel; 9. gearshift; 10. engine; 11. headlight; 12. bumper; 13. muffler; 14. battery

Something's Fishy

Surf's Up
1. beach umbrella is inside out; 2. lifeguard is facing the wrong way; 3. man in water is dressed in evening wear; 4. fisher is fishing with a rake; 5. skier is skiing without a boat; 6. people warming up at a campfire; 7. golfer on the beach; 8. people playing volleyball with a football; 9. sailboat has an upside-down sail; 10. in-line skater on the sand

Wacky Water park
1. park hours on sign are only at night; 2. no rungs on slide ladder; 3. alligator in the fountain; 4. pterodactyl in the sky; 5. inner tube slide spills out onto a golf tee; 6. big pair of glasses on the inner tube slide ramp; 7. queen in the lifeguard chair; 8. ice skater skating on the pool; 9. bed in the pool; 10. playing card lying on the deck; 11. herd of sheep in the picnic area

on the right track

bloomers
1. buttercup; 2. pansy; 3. snapdragon; 4. carnation; 5. foxglove; 6. daisy; 7. cowslip; 8. goldenrod

Pathways
Michelle should take trail 1, Juan trail 2, and Keisha trail 3.

Winter Vacation Crossword Puzzle

Mini-mystery: Highway Robbery

The man in the convertible wasn't telling the truth because he couldn't have driven from Salt Lake City in Utah to Chattanooga in Tennessee in 12 hours.

Happy Camper?

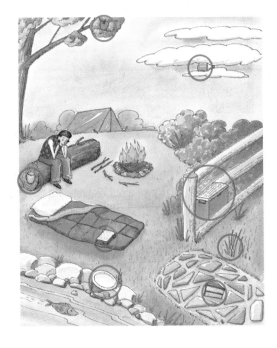

Message in the sand

"Say this three times fast: She sells seashells by the seashore."

Barnyard Scramble

1. dog; 2. cat; 3. cow; 4. toad; 5. duck; 6. goat; 7. crow; 8. goose; 9. mouse; 10. horse; 11. robin; 12. rabbit; 13. raccoon; 14. squirrel

Wait for me!

The race is On!

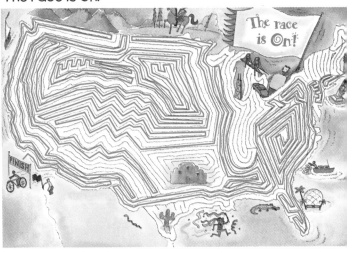

Movie Set Match-up

1. F; 2. G; 3. E; 4. D; 5. H; 6. A; 7. I; 8. C; 9. B; 10. J

Plane Challenge

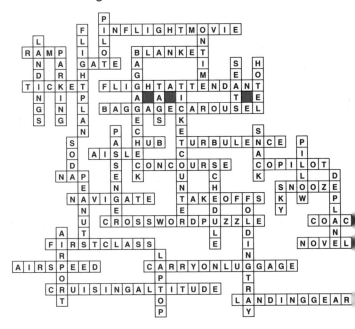

Bicycle Mix-up

1. large bike's seat is backwards; 2. yield sign is upside-down; 3. spokes missing on small bike; 4. center line on road is weaving; 5. tree growing in middle of road; 6. zebra; 7. airplane flying upside-down; 8. sun in front of cloud; 9. cow in distance is as big as the house; 10. no straps on backpack

Buy & Buy

You can buy a necklace, polished rock, postcard, wind-up toy, and candy for exactly 205 tickets.

Which hotel?

The Sleep Inn is the correct hotel.